Southbourne Library
Seabourne F
Southbourne
Tel: 01202

D0539572

16. MAR

BOURNEMOUTH LIBRARIES

620125496 Z

BOURNEMOUTH LIBRARIES	
620125496 Z	
C827	£3.99
2008	PETERS
SO	

First published in the UK by HarperCollins Children's Books in 2008

1 3 5 7 9 10 8 6 4 2

ISBN 978-0-00-728737-6

A CIP catalogue record for this title is available from the British Library.

No part of this publication may be reproduced, stored in a retrieval system or
transmitted in any form or by any means, electronic, mechanical, photocopying,
recording or otherwise, without the prior permission of HarperCollins Publishers
Ltd, 77-85 Fulham Palace Road, Hammersmith, London W6 8JB.

www.harpercollins.co.uk

Basil Brush®: © 2008 Ivan Owen's Estate and Peter Firmin under exclusive licence

Very NAUGHTY JOKE BOOK

Animal Antics

What did the monkey say when it got into a hot bath?
Oooh-oooh-oooh-aaah-aaah-aaah!

What do you call a chicken that's been run over by a truck?
Coq au Van!

Who are the moodiest animals in the zoo?
Camels – they've always got the hump!

What do you call a pig with three eyes?
Piiig!

Why don't owls go on dates when it rains?
Because it's too wet to woo!

Why did the hedgehog cross the road?
To visit its flat mate!

What do you get when you cross a rotten egg with a giant gorilla?
King Pong!

What newspaper do cats read?
Mews of the World!

What did the beaver say when it swam into a wall?
Dam!

What do you give a sick bird?
Tweetment!

What did the spider do on the internet?
Make a website.

Why did the bald man paint rabbits on his head?
Because from a distance they looked like hares.

What do you call a cow eating grass?
A lawn-mooer!

How do you fix a broken chimpanzee?
With a monkey wrench!

What's big, grey and flies straight up?
An elecopter!

What goes "snap, crackle and pop"?
A firefly with a short circuit!

How long do chickens work?
Around the cluck!

What books do owls like?
Hoot-dunits!

What day do fish hate?
Fry-day!

Cousin Mortimer's
Old Skool Rude Jokes!

Shield your eyes, my Brushingtons. Here comes my sneaky cousin Mortimer's set of burp-inducing jokes! Cover your ears, hide your cat and get ready to be grossed-out!

Why did the tide turn?
Because the sea-weed!

What did one toilet say to the other?
You're flushed.

My friend is built upside down...
His nose runs, and his feet smell!

Why did the toilet roll down the hill?
Because it wanted to get to the bottom!

> *What's big, red, and might kill you if it fell out*
> *of an apple tree as you walked underneath?*
> A combine harvester.

Did you hear about the cannibal who was late for
the dinner party?
He was given the cold shoulder!

> *How do you make a tissue dance?*
> Put some bogey into it!

What's green and hangs off trees?
Giraffe snot.

That's enough of Cousin Mortimer's smelly riddles. You don't want to puke on your hamster!

Unless you want one more? Oh, well, if you must insist, the Brush will deliver!

Basil, Dave and Anil were walking through the jungle when they came to a giant pot with a huge slide in it. There was a magic wizard standing next to the pot. When they approached the wizard, he said: "When you shoot down the slide, shout out your favourite thing in the whole world and the pot will fill with your requested substance and you will land in it!" So, Basil went down the slide shouting "jelly babies!". Dave went down the slide shouting, "money!". When Anil whizzed down the slide he shouted, "weeeeeeeeeeeeeeee!"... !

BOOM! BOOM!

Freaky Food by Bingo Brush

Introducing you to my joke-tastic nephew – Bingo Brush! Fresh from the Brush family tree, he is bringing you this randominski selection of culinary jokes! Bingo, it's over to you, young fox. . .

Greetings, fellow joke lovers! Set your greasy chops around my giggle-busting jokes! These will beat Basil and Mortimer's efforts any day!

Waiter! Waiter! This egg is bad.
Don't blame me, I only laid the table.

What do cannibals do at weddings?
Toast the bride and groom!

What's red, and flies and wobbles at the same time?
A jelly-copter!

What's that fly doing in my gravy?
It looks like front crawl to me!

What came after the stone age and the bronze age?
The sausage!

What did the snake say when it was offered some cheese?
Thanks, I'll just have a small slither.

What's the difference between school dinners and a load of slugs?
School dinners come on a plate!

What's the fastest food in the World?
Scone!

Why are there no French bakeries in the jungle?
Because elephants never baguette.

What do policeman eat?
Irish stew, Irish stew in the name of the law.

What did one fish say to the other fish?
I've haddock up to here with you!

Why did the tomato blush?
Because it saw the salad dressing!

What did the teddy bear say when he was offered dessert?
No thanks, I'm stuffed!

Why did the man at the orange juice factory lose his job?
He couldn't concentrate!

What kind of lettuce did they serve on the Titanic?
Iceberg!

What do you call two banana peels?
A pair of slippers!

What did the mother ghost tell the baby ghost when he ate too fast?
Stop goblin your food.

Why are chefs hard to like?
Because they beat eggs, whip cream, and mash potatoes!

Where do burgers like to dance?
At a Meatball!

Why did the man go into the pizza business?
He wanted to make some dough.

What do you call cheese that isn't yours?
Nacho cheese!

How do you make a milk shake?
Give it a good scare!

Now, that's enough of Bingo's jokes for now. Join your host for the next set of tonsil ticklers!

Basil's Barmy Jokes

What do you call a man with a spade on his head?
Doug.

> *What do you call a man without a spade on his head?*
> Doug-less.

What do you call a man with a toilet on his head?
Lou.

> *What do you call a man with a car on his head?*
> Jack.

What do you call a man who loves rabbits?
Warren.

BOOM! BOOM!

It's the way I tell 'em, Brushingtons!

How do you keep an idiot in suspense?
I'll tell you tomorrow.

What sort of vegetables can you grow in your basement?
Cellar-y!

What noise does a rapper's phone make?
Bling, bling! Bling, bling!

Why did the teacher put the classroom lights on?
Because the pupils were so dim!

What city cheats at exams?
Peking!

How was the Roman Empire cut in half?
With a pair of Caesars!

*What did Cinderella say when her photos
did not show up?*
Someday my prints will come!

What colour is a burp?
Burple!

What type of bird do people eat at every meal?
Swallow!

Ever wanted to know my TOP SECRET for making people laugh until their tonsils ache?

Just follow my 3 step plan, and the comical world can be yours.

STEP ONE
Tell a funny joke

STEP TWO
Wait for 1.5 seconds and then shout
'Boom! Boom!' at the top of your lungs

STEP THREE
Laugh raucously at your own joke!

Well, it works for me!
He he!

Goosebumps and Creepy Croaks

What do monsters make with cars?
Traffic jam.

Where do Aliens keep their sandwiches?
In a launch box.

What streets do ghosts haunt?
Dead ends!

What's a vampire's favourite sport?
Batminton.

What's Dracula's car called?
A mobile blood unit!

A boy went to a Halloween party with a sheet on his head. "Are you a ghost?" asked his friends.
"No, I'm an unmade bed!"

What do skeletons say before they begin dining?
Bone appetit!

Where do baby ghosts go during the day?
Dayscare centres.

What does a skeleton order at a restaurant?
Spare ribs!

Who did the ghost invite to his party?
Anyone he could dig up!

What did the skeleton say while riding his motorcycle?
I'm bone to be wild!

Why are graveyards so noisy?
Because of all the coffin!

What did one vampire say to the other?
Fangs aren't what they used to be.

What does Mrs Dracula say to Mr Dracula when he goes out to work in the evening?
Have a nice bite!

What did the french fries dress up as for Halloween?
Masked potatoes.

Why do vampires clean their teeth three times a day?
To prevent bat breath!

Don't Let Me Down

Introducing the mightiest joke of the century!
My booms were made for this tonsil tickling
extravaganza! Enjoy!

*What did the inflatable teacher say to
the inflatable pupil at the inflatable
school after she caught him with a pin?
You've let me down, you've let yourself down
and you've let the whole school down!*

BOOM! BOOM!

He! He!
Beat that one, Mortimer!

Sock One to Me, Foxy Fans!

It is now over to you to turn my cheeks pink and make the world shake with Booms! After setting a special joke competition, we have selected the lucky people named below as my funniest fans, EVER! Enjoy!

How did the farmer count his cows?
He used a COWculator!
Edin O'Brien

What's orange and sounds like a parrot?
A carrot!
Nathaniel Comerford

Did you hear about the baker who got a shock?
He was making some buns when a currant went up his trouser leg!
Daniel Bayley

What's black, white and red all over?
A sunburnt zebra!
Caitlin Holloway

The worms went into Noah's Ark in an apple-
They weren't happy as they were supposed
to go in pears!
Isabella Norman

Why did the chef get arrested?
Because he'd beaten up an egg.
Ollie Garvie

Where did the monkey cook his toast?
Under the gorilla.
Roisin Cullen

Knock Knock!
Who's There?
Amos
Amos Who?
A mosquito bit me.

Knock Knock!
Who's There?
Andy
Andy Who?
Andy bit me again!

George Hazell

Why did the squirrel scream?
Because someone pinched his nuts.
James & Megan Tomline

What do you call a penguin in the jungle?
Lost.
Phillip Bull

What is a cow's favourite building?
A MOO-seum!
Cara Ellaway

It's raining cats and dogs!
I know, I just stepped in a poodle!
Osian Morris

What's 300 feet tall and wobbly?
The Trifle Tower.
Aled Kite

What do you get if you cross a cow with a kangaroo?
I don't know but you'd need to milk it on a pogo stick.
Oliver Vobe

I sat up all night wondering where the sun had gone.
Suddenly, it dawned on me!
Ella Krisson

Why couldn't the leopard escape from the zoo?
Because he was always spotted!
Daniel Rose

Why did the banana go to the hospital?
Because he wasn't peeling very well.
Max Richards

Did you put the cat out?
Why, was it on fire?
Jake Huckle

What do you call a witch's motorcycle?
A brrrrooomstick.
Rhys Parfitt

What do you call a monster on the end of your finger?
A Bogeyman.
Shannon Hammond

Why did the dinosaur cross the road?
Because the chicken hadn't evolved yet.
Joe Oliver Tucker

What do you get if you cross a sheep and a kangaroo?
A woolly jumper.
Charlotte Ellingham

Double Acts

Two aerials meet on a roof, fall in love and get married.
The ceremony wasn't much but the reception was brilliant.

Why don't skeletons fight each other?
They don't have the guts.

What do you get when you cross a cat with a lemon?
A sour puss!

School's Out!

I would keep these jokes hidden far from your teacher's prying eyes. . .Did I ever tell you I was a real teacher's pet when I went to school back in the day? They kept me in a cage in the staffroom!

BOOM! BOOM!

Sir Sir, my pen's run out!
Run after it then!

A pupil came home from school seeming rather depressed.
"What's the matter, son?" asked his mother.
"It's my marks," said the boy. "They're all wet."
"What do you mean 'all wet'?"
"I mean," he replied, "below C-level."

Why were the teacher's eyes crossed?
She couldn't control her pupils!

> *Teacher: Why does your geography exam have a big zero over it?*
> Pupil: It's not a zero, the teacher ran out of stars, so she gave me a moon instead!

What do you call a pig studying karate?
A pork chop.

> *What kind of food do maths teachers eat?*
> Square meals!

Teacher: You aren't paying attention to me. Are you having trouble hearing?
Pupil: No, teacher, I'm having trouble listening!

Teacher: Did your parents help you with these homework problems?
Pupil: No, I got them wrong all by myself!

Who was the biggest thief in history?
Atlas, he held up the whole world!

Teacher: Why are you doing your maths sums on the floor?
Pupil: You told me to do it without using tables!

What's the difference between a teacher and a steam train?

The first goes "Spit out that chewing gum immediately!" and the second goes "chew chew"!

A little girl came home from school and said to her mother, "*Mummy, today in school I was punished for something that I didn't do.*"

The mother exclaimed, "*But that's terrible! I'm going to have a talk with your teacher about this ... by the way, what was it that you didn't do?*"

The little girl replied, "*My homework.*"

Froggy Humour

A frog walked into a bank and asked a man called Patty for a loan.

Patty said, 'Well, sir, we can't give you a loan.'

'Why not?' asked the frog.

'Well,' said Patty. 'You're a frog.'

'I'd like to see the manager of the bank,' said the frog.

So Patty went and got the manager. 'What seems to be the problem?' asked the manager.

'Patty says I can't have a loan because I'm a frog.'

'Well, do you have money?' asked the manager. The frog pulled a small glass elephant out of his pocket. 'What is that!?' exclaimed Patty. The manager said, 'It's a Knick-Knack, Patty.' Whack!!! 'Give the frog a loan.'

Mortimer and Bingo's Knock Knock Naughties!

Mortimer: Knock knock.

Bingo: Who's there?

Mortimer: Justin.

Bingo: Justin who?

Mortimer: Justin time for dinner!

Mortimer: Knock knock.

Bingo: Who's there?

Mortimer: Yah!

Bingo: Yah who?

Mortimer: Ride 'em, cowboy!

Mortimer: Knock knock.

Bingo: Who's there?

Mortimer: Juicy.

Bingo: Juicy who?

Mortimer: Juicy that rude sign on the door!

Mortimer: Knock knock.
Bingo: Who's there?
Mortimer: Gorilla.
Bingo: Gorilla who?
Mortimer: Gorilla me a hamburger!

Mortimer: Knock knock.
Bingo: Who's there?
Mortimer: Anita.
Bingo: Anita who?
Mortimer: Anita you like a hole in the head!

Mortimer: Knock knock.
Bingo: Who's there?
Mortimer: Alec.
Bingo: Alec who?
Mortimer: Alec to burp everyday!

Bedroom Bananas

Why did the boy tiptoe past the medicine cabinet?
He didn't want to wake the sleeping pills!

*Why did the spaceship land outside
your bedroom?*
I must have left the landing light on!

Why did Granny put wheels on her rocking chair?
Because she wanted to Rock n' Roll.

*Why did the man take a ruler to bed
with him?*
To see how long he could sleep!

*Why is getting up at the crack of dawn like
a pig's tail?*
Because it is twirly!

What did the blanket say to the bed?
You are undercover!

Mum, I don't think I should go to school today. Since I woke up my head's been spinning and the room's going round and round!
Wow, you must have slept like a top!

Doctor, doctor, I walk in my sleep!
Don't forget to take some money for the bus home, then!

My older brother hasn't slept for days!
Really? Why's that?
Because he sleeps at night!

Did you hear the story about the mechanic who slept under an old truck?
He wanted to wake up oily in the morning!

Ah – sleep is such a wonderful thing, it's a shame you can't stay awake to enjoy it! I remember once I had a terrible problem with snoring. I snored so loudly I used to wake myself up. . . So I solved the problem by sleeping in the next room. Ha ha!

BOOM! BOOM!

Dr Danger Brush

Introducing the mightiest medicated doctor jokes straight from Dr Brush's mouth! I'll make you howl like a monkey. . . I'm a doctor. Trust me.
He he!

Doctor, Doctor, I keep thinking I'm a bell.
Take this medicine and if it doesn't work, give me a ring.

Doctor, Doctor, I feel like a biscuit.
You must be crackers.

Doctor, Doctor, I think I need glasses.
You certainly do, sir, this is a flower shop!

Doctor, Doctor, I feel like a king.
What's your name?
Joe.
You must be Joe King!

Doctor, Doctor, I feel like a pair of curtains.
Pull yourself together!

Doctor, Doctor, I think I'm a needle!
I see your point!

Doctor, Doctor, I can't get to sleep.
Lie on the edge of the bed, you'll soon drop off.

Doctor, Doctor, I feel like a pack of cards.
I'll deal with you later!

*Did you hear about the man who swallowed
Christmas decorations?*
He got tinselitis!

Doctor, Doctor, I keep thinking I'm a clock.
OK, just relax. There's no need to get wound
up about it.

What did the vampire doctor say to his patients?
Necks please!

Doctor, Doctor, I feel as if I'm getting smaller.
You'll just have to be a little patient.

Doctor, Doctor, people keep ignoring me.
Who said that?

*Doctor, Doctor I've got wind! Can you give
me something?*
Yes – here's a kite!

Cousin Mortimer must have been to visit the doctor.
Looks like a bad case of the windy pops is heading
my way! Time to turn over before he gasses us all out!

RUDE ALERT RUDE ALERT RUDE ALERT!

What's brown and smelly and sounds like a church bell?
Dung!

If you're American and you go into the toilet and American when you come out of the toilet, what are you when you're in the toilet?
European!

RUDE ALERT RUDE ALERT RUDE ALERT!

What has a bottom at the top?
Your legs!

Did you hear the joke about the fart?
You don't want to – it stinks!

What do you call someone who wipes his nose on his sleeve?
Green sleeves.

Why do gorillas have big nostrils?
Because they have big fingers to pick them!

What has four wheels and flies?
A rubbish truck!

A man went to the dentist and the dentist said: "Say ah!" The man said:"Why?" and the dentist said: "Because my dog died!"

BOOM! BOOM!

When Bingo Brush was in an English lesson, he asked the teacher if he could go to the bathroom. The teacher said yes but before he went, he had to say the alphabet. So he began reciting: "a,b,c,d,e,f,g,h,i,j,k,l,m,n,o,q,r,s,t,u,v,w,x,y,z." The teacher said, "but where is the p?" and Bingo replied, "It's running down my leg, miss!"

BOOM! BOOM!

Ooops – I hope Bingo doesn't realise I've snuck that one in! Sssshh – let's get on with the show!

Desert Island Mayhem

Three boys, stranded on a desert island, find a magic lantern containing a genie. The genie grants them each one wish. The first boy wishes he was off the island and back home – and poof!, he is back home. The second boy wishes the same thing – and poof!, he is gone too. The third guy says, "I'm lonely. I wish my friends were back here."

He! He! You have to laugh. . . although not if I were stuck on a desert island with Mortimer!

Gross Café Jokes

Jokes fresh from Anil's Café . . .

Waiter, Waiter! There is a fly in my soup.
I'm sorry, sir, the dog must have missed it.

Why do cannibals eat clowns?
Because they taste funny!

What do mermaids have on toast?
Mermalade.

Why was the chef in a bad mood?
Because he had a chip on his shoulder!

A man walks into a pub and says, "Do you have any helicopter flavour crisps?".
"No, Sir" the barman replies. "We only have PLANE!"

Waiter, Waiter! My food tastes funny.
Then why aren't you laughing?

Waiter, Waiter! There's a slug in my soup.
Sorry, no pets allowed!

Why are eggs such losers?
Because they are always getting beaten!

Smelly Slimers

Hold your noses fellow fox lovers! This set of stinky jokes has been pulled from the bottom of Mortimer's dirty sock drawer! Pooo!

What happens when you play table tennis with a rotten egg?
First it goes ping, then it goes pong!

What do you call a skunk that flies?
A smellicopter!

Why do giraffes have such long legs?
Because they don't like the smell of their feet!

What would you get if you crossed a skunk and a sheep?
A furry animal that smells really baaaad!

What did one stinky toilet say to the other?
You look a little flushed!

How many rotten eggs does it take to make a really bad smell?
Only a phew!

What do you call a man with cow droppings all over his feet?
An incowpoop!

What do you get if you cross a crocodile with a flower?
I don't know, but I'm not going to smell it!

Vampire Hoo Ha!

A vampire bat came flapping in from the night covered in fresh blood. He joined the rest of the bats at the top of the cave to get some sleep. Pretty soon all the other bats could smell the blood and began asking him where he got it. The vampire bat told them to shut up and let him get some sleep but they persisted until finally he gave in. "OK, follow me," he said and flew out of the cave with hundreds of bats behind him. Down through a valley they went, over a river and into a forest full of trees. Finally he slowed down and all the other bats excitedly milled around him. "Now, do you see that tree over there?" he asked. "Yes, yes, yes!" the bats all screamed in a frenzy. "Good," said the vampire bat, "Because I DIDN'T!"

BOOM! BOOM!

One of my all time favourites!

Silly Jokes

What do you call a French man in sandals?
Philippe Floppe!

Why did the one-handed man cross the road?
To get to the second-hand shop!

Why did the bunny cross the road?
Because he wanted to show his girlfriend
he could hip hop!

Did you hear the one about the London Marathon?
My friend, Angelica was taking part. I was going
to help her. I bought her a pair of running shoes –
only trouble was, she couldn't keep up with them!

Why are football pitches always wet?
Because the players dribble so much!

> *Why did the snowman send his dad to the North Pole?*
> Because he wanted frozen pop!

One cow said to the other cow, "About this mad cow disease, it's a bit worrying, isn't it?"
The other cow said, "I'm not worried at all, I'm a duck!"

> *What do sheep do on sunny days?*
> Have a baa - baa - cue!

What do moths study at school?
Mothomatics!

How many donkeys can you fit on a fire engine?
One on the right, one on the left, and one on the top saying 'eeoh eeoh'.

> *Why did the golfer wear two pairs of trousers?*
> In case he got a hole in one!

What did the biscuit say when he got run over?
Oh, crumbs!

> *What is yellow and dangerous?*
> Shark infested custard!

What do you get if you cross a cow and a stereo?
A moooooosical!

Smelly Sport

As you know, I have never been one for
overexerting myself on the games pitch but
I know how to tell a sporty joke or two!
Feast your eyes on this set of crackers!

*Did you hear about the marathon runner
who worked as a chimney sweep?*
He was a great runner but suffered from
Athlete's Soot!

*Why was Cinderella thrown off the basketball
team?*
Because she ran away from the ball.

Old skiers never die. They just go downhill.

*What's the difference between a dog and
a football player?*
One drools, the other one dribbles.

What kind of cat likes to go bowling?
An alley cat.

Why did the golfer have an extra pair of pants?
In case he got a hole-in-one.

Why can't you play sports in the jungle?
Because of all the cheetahs.

Why was Cinderella such a bad football player?
Because her coach was a pumpkin.

What do you call a boomerang that doesn't work?
A stick.

Why did the basketball player go to prison?
Because he shot the ball.

What is the hardest part of skydiving?
The ground.

Now it's your turn to create your naughtiest jokes!

Mortimer has given you five different themes. Just write the funniest joke you can think of in the space and join our giggle munching gang!

FOOD

ANIMALS

SCHOOL

FAMILY

RUDE!

Goodbye for now,
my fellow joke busters!

Attention Class!

Join us for an unforgettable lesson in Madness, Mayhem and Mess!
Basil will be helped by a spectacular supporting "class" in a Skool-tastic adventure with gallons of giggles guaranteed

Don't miss Basil Brush's "High Skool Mani...
In a class of its own! Boom Boom!

2008

Sat 20th September	Medina Theatre, Newport, I-O-W	01983 527020
Sun 21st September	The Capitol, Horsham	01403 750220
Sat 27th September	Royal Spa Centre, Leamington Spa	01926 334418
Sun 28th September	Loughborugh Town Hall	01509 231914
Sat 4th October	Kings Theatre, Southsea	023 9282 8282
Sun 5th October	Lighthouse, Poole	0844 406 8666
Sat 11th October	The Albert Halls, Bolton	01204 334400
Sun 12th October	Playhouse Arts Centre, Alnwick	01665 510785
Sat 18th October	Dorking Halls, Dorking	01306 881717
Sun 19th October	Broadway Theatre, Catford	020 8690 0002
Sat 25th October	Charter Theatre, Preston	0845 344 2012
Mon 27th October	Villa Marina, Douglas, Isle Of Man	01624 694555
Tues 28th October	forum28, Barrow In Furness	01229 820000
Wed 29th October	Ashcroft Theatre, Croydon	020 8688 9291
Thur 30th October	The Lowry, Salford Quays	0870 787 5790
Fri 31st October	Palace Theatre, Newark	01636 655755
Sat 1st November	Alban Arena, St Albans	01727 844488
Sun 2nd November	Central Theatre, Chatham	01634 338338
Sat 8th November	Playhouse Theatre, Weston Super Mare	01934 645544
Sun 9th November	Journal Tyne Theatre, Newcastle Upon Tyne	0844 493 9999
Sat 15th November	Winter Gardens, Margate	01843 296111
		01843 292795

Also coming to a theatre near you February - May 2009

Don't Miss Basil In Panto!
At the Ipswich Regent Theatre
12th December 2008 - 4th January 2009
Box Office: 01473 433100

Buy tickets online at www.basilbrush.com

RIGHTS